THE COMPLETE

LAS VEGAS TRAVEL GUIDE

2023

"Sin City Shenanigans"

From High Stakes to High Heels: The Ultimate Guide to Unforgettable Adventures in the Entertainment Capital

DENBY DOUGH

Copyright © 2023 by Denby Dough

All rights reserved. No part of this publication may be reproduced, distributed, or transmitted in any form or by any means, including photocopying, recording, or other electronic or mechanical methods, without the prior written permission of the publisher, except in the case of brief quotations embodied in critical reviews and certain other non-commercial uses permitted by copyright law.

This book is a work of non-fiction. While the author has made every effort to provide accurate and up-to-date information, neither the publisher nor the author can be held responsible for any errors or omissions. The information contained in this book is intended for educational and informational purposes only.

Table of Contents

Introduction:

Welcome to the Neon Playground

Welcome to Las Vegas, the vibrant and electrifying city that never sleeps! Get ready to immerse yourself in a world where the boundaries of reality blur and dreams come true.

See, Las Vegas is not just a destination; it's an experience unlike any other. From the moment you step foot on the infamous Las Vegas Strip, you'll be greeted by a spectacle of flashing lights, towering hotels, and cascading fountains that will leave you in awe.

Sin City embraces excess and revels in its own audacity. Here, you can witness the marvels of modern architecture, catch world-class performances, and try your luck at the glittering casinos that dot the landscape.

But again, Las Vegas is more than just bright lights and high stakes. It's a city of endless possibilities, where you can find hidden gems nestled in the heart of downtown.

Or you can venture beyond the Strip to discover the natural wonders that surround this desert oasis. Whether you're a foodie seeking culinary delights, a fashionista in search of the latest trends, or a thrill-seeker looking for adrenaline-pumping adventures, Las Vegas has something for everyone.

In this travel guide, I've compiled a comprehensive collection of insider knowledge, local secrets, and practical tips to help you navigate the exhilarating world of Las Vegas. The guide will show you where to find the best entertainment, introduce you to the most delectable dining experiences, and unveil the city's hidden treasures that only the savviest of travelers know about.

But be warned: Las Vegas is a city that can be both captivating and overwhelming. It's a place where time seems to stand still, and the line between fantasy and reality blurs. As you explore the city, remember to pace yourself, stay hydrated, and always keep an eye on the clock – because in Las Vegas, the hours can slip away like chips at a roulette table.

Now, fasten your seatbelt, adjust your sunglasses, and get ready to embark on an unforgettable adventure through the glittering streets of Las Vegas. Let "Sin City Shenanigans" be your trusted companion as you navigate this neon playground, ensuring that you make the most of your visit and create memories that will last a lifetime.

WELCOME
TO Fabulous
LAS VEGAS
NEVADA

Chapter 1:

A Roll of the Dice: Navigating the Strip and Downtown

Welcome to the first chapter of your personalized guide to Las Vegas! In this chapter, let me be your trusted companion as we navigate the bustling streets of the Strip and uncover the hidden gems of downtown.

From deciphering the glittering maze of Las Vegas Boulevard to immersing ourselves in the vibrant energy of the Fremont Street Experience, get ready for an adventure like no other. Oh, and don't worry—I've got some insider tips up my sleeve to ensure you can get around this dazzling city with ease. So, let's dive right in!

Decoding the Glittering Maze: A Guide to Las Vegas Boulevard

Las Vegas Boulevard, commonly known as the Strip, is the beating heart of the city.

It stretches for miles, lined with iconic hotels, larger-than-life resorts, and an array of dazzling attractions. Navigating this glittering maze can be a bit overwhelming, but fear not—I'm here to guide you through it all.

From the wonder of the Luxor to the iconic dancing fountains of the Bellagio, you'll find out the must-see landmarks, with tips on navigating the bustling sidewalks, and uncovering the hidden gems tucked away between the flashy facades.

What Not to Miss on The Strip

As a visitor to Las Vegas, the Las Vegas Strip is the heart of the city's entertainment and attractions. Here are some main attractions you shouldn't miss on the Strip:

The Welcome to Fabulous Las Vegas Sign:

Kickstart your Las Vegas adventure with a visit to the iconic Welcome Sign. Located at the southern end of the Strip, this landmark is a perfect photo opportunity and a symbol of the city's warm hospitality.

Location: 5100 Las Vegas Blvd S, Las Vegas, NV

The Bellagio Fountains: Witness the mesmerizing water, music, and light show of the Bellagio Fountains. Located in front of the Bellagio Hotel, this iconic attraction offers spectacular displays every 30 minutes in the evenings.

Location: 600 S Las Vegas Blvd, Las Vegas, NV

The High Roller Observation Wheel: Take a ride on the High Roller, the world's tallest observation wheel. Located at The LINQ Promenade, this giant Ferris wheel offers stunning panoramic views of the Las Vegas Strip and the city skyline.

Location: 3545 S Las Vegas Blvd, Las Vegas, NV

The Venetian and The Palazzo: Explore the Venetian and The Palazzo resorts, which offer a taste of Venice with their beautifully recreated canals and gondola rides. Enjoy upscale shopping, fine dining, and immerse yourself in the grandeur of these luxurious resorts.

Location: 3325 S Las Vegas Blvd, Las Vegas, NV

The Mirage Volcano: Experience the eruption of The Mirage Volcano, a free outdoor spectacle featuring fire, water, and music. The volcano erupts nightly, creating a dramatic display that shouldn't be missed.

Location: 3400 S Las Vegas Blvd, Las Vegas, NV

The LINQ Promenade: Stroll through The LINQ Promenade, a lively outdoor entertainment district. Enjoy shopping, dining, and entertainment options, including the unique High Roller observation wheel and various bars.

Location: 3545 S Las Vegas Blvd, Las Vegas, NV

The Stratosphere Tower: Visit the Stratosphere Tower, an iconic Las Vegas landmark offering breathtaking views from its observation deck. Thrill-seekers can also try the exhilarating rides located at the top of the tower.

Location: 2000 Las Vegas Blvd S, Las Vegas, NV

The Eiffel Tower Experience: Take a trip to Paris without leaving Las Vegas by visiting the Eiffel Tower Experience at the Paris Las Vegas hotel.

Enjoy panoramic views of the Strip from the observation deck and capture memorable photos.

Location: 3655 S Las Vegas Blvd, Las Vegas, NV

The Neon Museum: Delve into the history of Las Vegas through its iconic neon signs at the Neon Museum. Take a guided tour and explore the collection of restored and illuminated neon signs that once adorned the city.

Location: 770 Las Vegas Blvd N, Las Vegas, NV

These are just a few of the many attractions you can explore on the Las Vegas Strip. From the dazzling resorts and casinos to the vibrant nightlife and entertainment options, there's something for everyone to enjoy in this bustling area.

Remember to check the specific opening hours and availability of attractions, as they may vary. It's also a good idea to plan your visits during weekdays or non-peak hours to avoid large crowds and long queues.

Downtown Delights: Exploring Fremont Street Experience

When you've had your fill of the Strip's grandeur, it's time to venture downtown and discover the vibrant energy of the Fremont Street Experience.

This historic district boasts a lively atmosphere, vintage casinos, and a captivating light show that will leave you in awe. I'll take you through the lively pedestrian mall, where street performers dazzle with their talents and local vendors offer unique treasures.

We'll explore the legendary Golden Nugget, immerse ourselves in the retro charm of the Neon Museum, and sample some mouthwatering bites at the popular Container Park. Get ready to embrace the electric vibe of downtown Las Vegas!

Here's what you need to know to make the most of your downtown exploration:

The Canopy Light Show: The Fremont Street Experience is famous for its dazzling Viva Vision Light Show. Every evening, a spectacular display of lights and music takes over the canopy-covered pedestrian mall. Make sure to catch one of the scheduled shows—it's a sight you won't want to miss!

Vintage Casinos and Neon Signage: Downtown Las Vegas is home to historic casinos with unique charm. Explore the Golden Nugget, Binion's, and Four Queens to experience the classic Vegas atmosphere. Don't forget to admire the vintage neon signage that adds a touch of nostalgia to the area.

Fremont East District: Beyond the Fremont Street Experience, the Fremont East District offers a hip and trendy scene with lively bars, restaurants, and entertainment venues. It's the perfect place to grab a drink, enjoy live music, or experience the vibrant nightlife.

Insider Tips for Getting Around: Taxis, Ride-Sharing, and Monorails

Now let's dive into some insider tips for getting around this sprawling city. Las Vegas offers a range of transportation options, and I'm here to help you navigate them like a pro.

Whether you prefer the convenience of taxis, or the unique experience of the monorail, in this guide, you'll get all the information you need to make informed decisions.

We'll discuss the best times to travel, tips for avoiding traffic, and how to navigate the city's transportation hubs seamlessly. With these tips, you'll spend less time worrying about logistics and more time immersing yourself in the excitement of Las Vegas.

To navigate Las Vegas efficiently, consider these insider tips for getting around the city:

Taxis and Ride-Sharing: Taxis are readily available throughout Las Vegas, and ride-sharing services like Uber and Lyft are also popular options.

Keep in mind that during peak times, such as weekends or major events, wait times for rides might be longer. It's advisable to have a backup plan or explore alternative transportation options.

Monorail: The Las Vegas Monorail offers a convenient way to travel between resorts on the Strip. The rail runs from the MGM Grand to the SLS Las Vegas, stopping at various resorts along the way. It operates from early morning until late at night, and you can purchase single-ride tickets, or multi-day passes to suit your needs.

Walking Distances: Las Vegas may appear smaller than it actually is, so be prepared for longer walking distances between resorts. Wearing comfortable shoes and staying hydrated will make your exploration more enjoyable.

Take Advantage of Pedestrian Walkways: Speaking of walking, the Strip is packed with pedestrian walkways that allow you to stroll comfortably between resorts and attractions. Utilize these walkways to avoid the heavy traffic and take in the sights at your own pace.

Familiarize Yourself with Landmarks: Get to know the iconic landmarks that define the Strip. From the Eiffel Tower at Paris Las Vegas to the replica canals of The Venetian, these landmarks can serve as your guiding points as you explore.

Best Times to Move Around in Sin City

To avoid heavy traffic in Las Vegas, it's helpful to plan your travel outside of peak hours and major events. Here are some tips for navigating the city with minimal traffic congestion:

Weekdays: Weekdays generally have less traffic compared to weekends, as many locals and tourists tend to visit during the weekends. If your schedule allows, plan your travel for Monday through Thursday.

Morning and Late Evening: Early mornings, before 7:00 AM, and late evenings, after 9:00 PM, typically experience lighter traffic.

This can be especially beneficial if you're traveling to or from the airport or heading to popular destinations along the Strip.

Avoid Rush Hours: Las Vegas experiences rush hours typically between 7:00 AM to 9:00 AM and 4:00 PM to 6:00 PM, when locals are commuting to and from work. Try to plan your travel outside of these peak hours to minimize traffic congestion.

Plan Around Events: Las Vegas hosts numerous events, conventions, and conferences throughout the year, which can significantly impact traffic. Check the event calendar for major gatherings and consider adjusting your travel plans accordingly.

Use Navigational Apps: Utilize navigation apps such as Google Maps or Waze to get real-time traffic updates and alternative route suggestions. These apps can help you navigate around congested areas and find the quickest routes.

Consider Public Transportation: Can never emphasize this enough. If you're staying on or near the Strip, utilizing the Las Vegas Monorail or the extensive RTC bus system can be a convenient and traffic-free option to explore the city.

Remember that traffic conditions can vary, so it's always a good idea to check for live traffic updates before heading out. Additionally, allow yourself extra time for travel, especially during peak periods, to ensure a stress-free journey.

Now that you have a grasp of how to navigate the Strip and downtown, you're ready to dive into the exciting world of Las Vegas entertainment in the next chapter. Get ready for captivating shows, electrifying performances, and non-stop fun! So, let's hit the streets and make the most of your time in Sin City!

Chapter 2:

Showtime Extravaganza: The Best Entertainment in Town

Welcome to Chapter 2 of your personalized guide to Las Vegas! In this chapter, we'll explore the dazzling world of entertainment that the city has to offer. From mesmerizing shows to side-splitting comedy, we'll ensure that your visit to Las Vegas is filled with unforgettable experiences.

So, let's get ready to be entertained. let's dive right in and discover where and when these amazing activities take place!

From Legends to Magic: Must-See Shows and Performances

Las Vegas is renowned for its world-class entertainment, featuring legendary performers and mind-bending magic acts. Here are some must-see shows and performances that will leave you spellbound:

Legends in Concert: Experience the magic of live tribute performances at Legends in Concert. From Elvis Presley to Frank Sinatra and beyond, this show brings the legends back to life with incredible impersonators who capture the essence of these iconic performers.

When/Where: This legendary tribute show takes place at the Tropicana Las Vegas. Check their schedule for showtimes and secure your tickets in advance to witness the awe-inspiring performances that pay homage to music's greatest icons.

Absinthe: Prepare to be amazed by the critically acclaimed variety show, Absinthe. Combining jaw-dropping acrobatics, hilarious comedy, and an intimate setting, this adults-only production pushes the boundaries of entertainment, leaving audiences in awe of its daring performances.

When/Where: Prepare for an unforgettable experience at the Absinthe Spiegeltent located at Caesars Palace.

Showtimes vary, so make sure to check the schedule and arrive early to secure your seat for this captivating, adults-only variety show.

Penn & Teller: Witness the comedic magic duo, Penn & Teller, as they blend illusions, humor, and skepticism in their long-running Las Vegas show. Known for their innovative tricks and engaging stage presence, they'll keep you entertained and guessing throughout the entire performance.

When/Where: Catch Penn & Teller's magic and comedy extravaganza at the Penn & Teller Theater inside the Rio All-Suite Hotel and Casino. Shows are typically scheduled on specific days, so plan ahead and book your tickets for an evening of mind-bending illusions and laughter.

Cirque du Soleil Unveiled: A Spectacular Showcase

No visit to Las Vegas would be complete without experiencing the awe-inspiring productions of Cirque du Soleil.

Known for their mesmerizing acrobatics, artistic storytelling, and breathtaking visuals, here are some Cirque du Soleil shows you shouldn't miss:

O: Dive into a world of water, acrobatics, and surreal beauty in the aquatic masterpiece, "O." Set in and around a 1.5-million-gallon pool, this show combines synchronized swimming, high dives, and mesmerizing performances to create an unforgettable experience.

Where/When: Immerse yourself in the aquatic wonderland of "O" at the Bellagio Hotel and Casino. Showtimes for this mesmerizing production can vary, so be sure to check the schedule and secure your tickets in advance to witness the awe-inspiring performances that seamlessly blend acrobatics and water elements.

Mystère: Be transported into a realm of imagination and wonder with Mystère. This long-running Cirque du Soleil show combines impressive athleticism, stunning costumes, and a captivating storyline to create a performance that will leave you enthralled from start to finish.

Where/When: Experience the magic of Mystère at Treasure Island. Showtimes are scheduled throughout the week, offering you the chance to witness the artistry, athleticism, and whimsical storytelling that make this Cirque du Soleil show an absolute must-see.

Michael Jackson ONE: Pay tribute to the King of Pop himself in Michael Jackson ONE. This electrifying show features the music and choreography of Michael Jackson, brought to life by a talented cast of performers. Get ready for a thrilling and nostalgic journey through the music and legacy of an icon.

Where/When: Head to the Mandalay Bay Resort and Casino to witness the electrifying tribute show, Michael Jackson ONE. With showtimes on select days, check the schedule and prepare to be enthralled by the spectacular choreography and iconic music of the King of Pop.

Comedy Clubs and Late-Night Laughter: Where to Find the Best Giggles

If you're in the mood for laughter and comedy, Las Vegas has got you covered. Check out these comedy clubs and venues that offer top-notch performances and a dose of late-night hilarity:

The Comedy Cellar: Located at the Rio All-Suite Hotel and Casino, The Comedy Cellar brings you a lineup of seasoned comedians and rising stars. Get ready for an evening filled with laughter as these talented comics tickle your funny bone with their wit and humor.

Where/When: The Comedy Cellar offers shows throughout the week. Check their schedule for specific showtimes and make your way to this intimate venue to enjoy a night of laughter with a lineup of talented comedians.

Brad Garrett's Comedy Club: Head over to the MGM Grand and catch a show at Brad Garrett's Comedy Club. This venue, hosted by the Emmy Award-winning comedian himself, showcases a variety of comedic talents, promising an evening of side-splitting laughter.

Where/When: Showtimes can vary, so check their schedule and prepare for an evening of hilarity hosted by the Emmy Award-winning comedian himself.

Laugh Factory: Located at the Tropicana Las Vegas, the Laugh Factory is a comedy institution known for hosting both established comedians and up-and-coming talents. With shows seven nights a week, you're guaranteed to find something that suits your sense of humor.

Where/When: Find yourself at the Tropicana Las Vegas to experience the Laugh Factory, where comedy shows are held seven nights a week. With both renowned comedians and up-and-coming talents taking the stage, you're guaranteed to find a show that suits your sense of humor.

Get ready to be entertained and let the laughter echo through the halls of Las Vegas! Navigating to these entertainment venues is a breeze. You can conveniently use taxis or ride-sharing services like Uber and Lyft to reach your desired destinations.

Additionally, many resorts and hotels offer shuttle services or are within walking distance of each other on the Strip. If you're exploring downtown, consider using the Las Vegas Monorail or simply enjoy a leisurely stroll to immerse yourself in the vibrant atmosphere.

In the next chapter, we'll explore the culinary delights that await you in this vibrant city. So, keep your appetite ready and prepare to indulge in a gastronomic adventure like no other!

Chapter 3:

A Culinary Adventure: Indulge in Las Vegas' Gastronomic Delights

Welcome to Chapter 3 of your personalized guide to Las Vegas! In this chapter, I'll be your culinary companion as we embark on a delectable journey through the vibrant dining scene of this city.

From celebrity chef restaurants to hidden gems, we'll explore the flavors that make Las Vegas a true gastronomic paradise. So, get ready to indulge your taste buds and let's delve into the culinary adventure that awaits!

Michelin Stars and Celebrity Chef

Haute Cuisine: Fine Dining Delights

Las Vegas is a haven for culinary excellence, boasting a lineup of world-class restaurants helmed by Michelin-starred chefs and celebrity culinary icons.

Prepare to be dazzled by exquisite flavors and impeccable service at these fine dining establishments:

Gordon Ramsay Steak: Located in the Paris Las Vegas, Gordon Ramsay Steak offers a modern take on the classic steakhouse experience. Savor perfectly cooked steaks and signature dishes crafted with Chef Ramsay's culinary expertise.

Joël Robuchon: Elevate your dining experience at Joël Robuchon, located in the MGM Grand. This Michelin-starred restaurant offers a refined menu showcasing exquisite French cuisine, meticulously prepared with the finest ingredients.

Twist by Pierre Gagnaire: Immerse yourself in culinary artistry at Twist, nestled within the Waldorf Astoria Las Vegas. Chef Pierre Gagnaire's innovative creations, inspired by French cuisine with a modern twist, will take you on a gastronomic adventure like no other.

Restaurant Guy Savoy: Immerse yourself in the culinary mastery of renowned chef Guy Savoy at his eponymous restaurant inside Caesars Palace. From the delicate flavors of his signature artichoke and black truffle soup to the decadent desserts, each bite is a revelation of culinary perfection.

CUT by Wolfgang Puck: Indulge in a steakhouse experience like no other at CUT, situated in The Venetian. Created by celebrity chef Wolfgang Puck, this modern twist on the classic steakhouse offers prime cuts of meat, innovative sides, and an ambiance that exudes sophistication and glamour.

Hidden Gems and Local Flavors: Off the Beaten Path

Beyond the glitz and glamour, Las Vegas is also home to hidden culinary gems that showcase local flavors and unique dining experiences. Don't miss these off-the-beaten-path treasures:

Lotus of Siam: Venture off the Strip to discover Lotus of Siam, a beloved Thai restaurant that has gained international acclaim. Prepare for a burst of flavors as you indulge in their authentic and mouthwatering dishes.

Location: 620 E Flamingo Rd, Las Vegas, NV

Esther's Kitchen: Located in the Arts District, Esther's Kitchen delights visitors with its farm-to-table concept and Italian-inspired cuisine. From house-made pastas to wood-fired pizzas, this charming eatery offers a cozy atmosphere and culinary delights that will leave you craving more.

Location: 130 S Casino Center Blvd STE 110, Las Vegas, NV 89104

Sparrow + Wolf: Experience the eclectic and adventurous menu at Sparrow + Wolf in the vibrant Chinatown district. Chef Brian Howard's creative dishes draw inspiration from global flavors, resulting in a one-of-a-kind dining experience that pushes boundaries and surprises the palate.

Location: 4480 Spring Mountain Rd #100, Las Vegas, NV

Buffets and Brunches: Indulge in Las Vegas' Feast Culture

Las Vegas is synonymous with extravagant buffets and indulgent brunches. Here are a few places where you can revel in the city's feast culture:

Bacchanal Buffet: Set within Caesars Palace, the Bacchanal Buffet is a feast for the senses. With a wide array of international cuisines, including seafood, prime rib, and delectable desserts, this buffet is a must-visit for food enthusiasts.

Location: Caesars Palace, 3570 S Las Vegas Blvd, Las Vegas, NV

The Wicked Spoon: Located at The Cosmopolitan, The Wicked Spoon offers a sophisticated twist on traditional buffet dining. Feast on a diverse selection of globally inspired dishes served in individual portions, allowing you to sample a wide variety of flavors.

Location: The Cosmopolitan of Las Vegas, The Chelsea Tower, 3708 S Las Vegas Blvd Level 2, Las Vegas, NV

Bouchon Bistro: Treat yourself to a luxurious brunch

experience at Bouchon Bistro, situated at The Venetian. Indulge in classic French dishes, such as fluffy omelets, buttery pastries, and delightful crepes, all expertly prepared to perfection.

Location: The Venetian Las Vegas. 355 Las Vegas Blvd S 10th Floor, Las Vegas, NV

Sinfully Sweet: Desserts and Unique Culinary Experiences

No culinary adventure is complete without satisfying your sweet tooth. Las Vegas takes dessert to a whole new level, offering unique and indulgent experiences that will leave you in a state of pure bliss. Here are some sinfully sweet destinations you won't want to miss:

Milk Bar: Located at The Cosmopolitan, Milk Bar is a dessert lover's dream come true. Indulge in their signature treats like crack pie, cereal milk soft serve, and inventive cookies that push the boundaries of flavor and nostalgia.

The Chocolate Fountain at Bellagio: Immerse yourself in a chocolate lover's paradise at the Bellagio. Witness the spectacle of a towering chocolate fountain, where cascades of velvety chocolate tempt you to dip fruits, pastries, and more. It's a sweet experience that will awaken your senses.

Navigating the culinary landscape of Las Vegas is a pleasure, as many restaurants are conveniently located within hotels and resorts along the Strip. Whether you're a food enthusiast or just looking to indulge in delicious flavors, Las Vegas offers an array of dining options to satisfy every palate.

From world-class fine dining establishments helmed by renowned celebrity chefs to casual eateries serving up delectable comfort food, the dining scene in Las Vegas is truly exceptional. So, get your palate ready and enjoy!

Chapter 4:

Lady Luck's Playground: Gambling and Casinos

Welcome to Chapter 4 of your personalized guide to Las Vegas! In this chapter, we'll immerse ourselves in the thrilling world of gambling and casinos that make this city a haven for those seeking excitement and a chance to test their luck.

Whether you're a seasoned gambler or a curious beginner, I'll be your guide as we explore the ins and outs of Las Vegas-style gaming. So, let's roll the dice and dive into Lady Luck's playground!

Casino 101: A Crash Course in Vegas-Style Gaming

If you're new to the world of gambling or simply need a refresher, this section will provide you with a crash course on Vegas-style gaming. Here's what you need to know:

Understand the Games: From blackjack and roulette to craps and baccarat, familiarize yourself with the rules and strategies of popular casino games. Whether you prefer cards, dice, or wheels, each game offers its unique thrills and potential rewards.

Get the Etiquette and Casino Culture: Learn about the etiquette and customs of casinos to ensure a smooth and enjoyable gaming experience. From tipping dealers to respecting table limits, embracing casino culture adds to the excitement and camaraderie among players.

Manage Your Bankroll: Set a budget and establish a bankroll management strategy to ensure responsible gambling. Knowing how much you're willing to spend and setting limits for each session will help you enjoy the games without breaking the bank.

Hidden Gems: Off-the-Strip Casinos Worth Exploring

While the iconic casinos on the Strip garner much attention, Las Vegas is also home to hidden gems that offer unique and intimate gambling experiences. Step off the beaten path and discover these off-the-Strip casinos:

Red Rock Casino Resort & Spa: Located in Summerlin, Red Rock Casino offers a sophisticated atmosphere with a wide range of gaming options, including slots, table games, and a poker room. Explore the elegant surroundings and enjoy the relaxed ambiance away from the hustle and bustle of the Strip.

Green Valley Ranch Resort Spa & Casino: Situated in Henderson, Green Valley Ranch provides a luxurious gaming experience in a tranquil setting. With an array of table games, slots, and a high-limit room, this off-Strip gem offers a retreat from the crowds with its upscale amenities.

The Orleans Hotel & Casino: Experience the charm of The Orleans, just a few minutes west of the Strip. This locals' favorite offers a vibrant casino floor with a variety of games, including poker, blackjack, and slots. Don't miss their lively poker tournaments and exciting promotions.

Slots, Tables, and Poker: Insider Strategies for Success

Whether you prefer the spinning reels of slot machines, the strategic play of table games, or the competitive nature of poker, here are some insider strategies to enhance your chances of success:

Slots: Familiarize yourself with the different types of slot machines and their payout percentages. Look for machines with higher RTP (Return to Player) percentages and consider betting maximum coins for a chance at larger jackpots.

Table Games: Learn basic strategies for popular table games like blackjack and roulette.

Understanding optimal play and making informed decisions can improve your odds of winning and enhance your overall gaming experience.

Poker: Sharpen your poker skills by studying the game's

strategies, hand rankings, and different variants. Practice patience, observe your opponents' behaviors, and utilize betting strategies to gain an edge at the poker table.

Remember, gambling should be enjoyed responsibly. Set limits, take breaks, and prioritize having fun over chasing winnings. Las Vegas offers a multitude of gaming options for every taste and skill level, ensuring that your casino experience is filled with excitement and entertainment.

Now that you have a better understanding of the world of gambling and casinos in Las Vegas, it's time to explore the next chapter, where we'll uncover the city's therapeutic retail shopping offers. Get ready for a dazzling adventure shopping in Sin City!

Chapter 5:

Retail Therapy: Shopping in Sin City

Welcome to Chapter 5 of your personalized guide to Las Vegas! In this chapter, we'll dive into the world of shopping in Sin City, where you can indulge your fashion cravings, discover unique souvenirs, and master the art of bargain hunting.

From luxury boutiques to quirky shops, Las Vegas offers a shopping experience like no other. So, grab your wallet and get ready for a dose of retail therapy!

Fashion-forward: Exploring Luxury Boutiques and Designer Outlets

Las Vegas is a fashion capital, attracting shoppers with its array of luxury boutiques and designer outlets. Whether you're looking for high-end fashion or seeking the thrill of finding a great deal, this section has got you covered.

Here are some must-visit destinations for fashion-forward individuals:

The Forum Shops at Caesars Palace: Step into a world of luxury at The Forum Shops, an iconic shopping destination on the Strip. Here, you'll find an impressive collection of high-end fashion brands, from Gucci and Louis Vuitton to Versace and Chanel. Explore the opulent corridors and indulge in a shopping spree fit for royalty.

Location: Caesars Palace. 3500 Las Vegas Blvd S, Las Vegas, NV

Fashion Show Mall: Immerse yourself in a fashion extravaganza at the Fashion Show Mall, located at the heart of the Strip. This sprawling mall features a mix of luxury brands, popular retailers, and a runway where live fashion shows take place. Discover the latest trends and shop 'til you drop in this stylish haven.

Location: 3200 Las Vegas Blvd S Ste. 600, Las Vegas, NV

Las Vegas North Premium Outlets: If you're on the hunt for designer bargains, head to the Las Vegas North Premium Outlets. This outdoor shopping center offers discounts on renowned brands like Michael Kors, Coach, and Calvin Klein. Score incredible deals and elevate your wardrobe without breaking the bank.

Location: 875 S Grand Central Pkwy, Las Vegas, NV

Souvenirs and Beyond: Quirky Shops and Unique Finds

Las Vegas is not only a shopper's paradise but also a treasure trove of quirky shops and unique souvenirs. Take a break from the mainstream and explore these offbeat destinations

Bonanza Gift Shop: Dive into the world's largest gift shop at Bonanza, located on the Strip. This iconic store offers a wide range of Las Vegas-themed souvenirs, from T-shirts and keychains to quirky collectibles. Find the perfect memento to remember your time in Sin City.

Location: 2400 S Las Vegas Blvd, Las Vegas, NV

Container Park: Experience a one-of-a-kind shopping adventure at Container Park in Downtown Las Vegas. This open-air shopping center features boutique stores housed in repurposed shipping containers. Discover locally made products, artisanal crafts, and one-of-a-kind finds that showcase the city's vibrant creative scene.

Location: 707 E Fremont St, Las Vegas, NV

Antique Alley: Step back in time and browse through Antique Alley, a cluster of antique shops located in the Arts District. From vintage clothing and retro accessories to unique home decor pieces, this hidden gem is a haven for antique enthusiasts and collectors.

Location: 1126 S Main St, Las Vegas, NV

The Art of Bargain Hunting: Tips for Savvy Shoppers

Ready to master the art of bargain hunting? Here are some tips and tricks to help you navigate the shopping scene in Las Vegas like a pro:

Timing is Key: Keep an eye out for seasonal sales, holiday promotions, and special events when retailers offer discounts and deals. Visit outlet malls during weekdays to avoid the crowds and score even better bargains.

Join Rewards Programs: Sign up for rewards programs and newsletters offered by your favorite stores. This way, you'll be the first to know about exclusive discounts, member-only sales, and upcoming promotions.

Explore Local Markets: Don't limit your shopping experience to malls and outlets. Check out local markets and farmer's markets where you can find unique handmade items, locally crafted goods, and fresh produce. Here are some recommended options to immerse yourself in the vibrant local food scene:

Downtown 3rd Farmers Market: Located in the heart of downtown Las Vegas, the Downtown 3rd Farmers Market is a popular destination for locals and visitors alike. Here, you'll find a diverse selection of fresh fruits, vegetables, herbs, locally produced honey, baked goods, and more.

The market also features live music, food vendors, and crafts, creating a lively and enjoyable atmosphere.

Las Vegas Farmers Market: With multiple locations throughout the city, the Las Vegas Farmers Market offers a convenient way to access fresh, locally sourced products. Explore their various locations, such as Bruce Trent Park Farmers Market, Gardens Park Farmers Market, or the Downtown Summerlin Farmers Market, and discover an array of seasonal produce, artisanal goods, gourmet food products, and handmade crafts.

Fresh52 Farmers and Artisan Market: Fresh52 operates several farmers markets in Las Vegas, focusing on providing fresh, organic, and sustainable products.

With locations in Sansone Park Place, Tivoli Village, and Skye Canyon, these markets offer a wide selection of farm-fresh fruits and vegetables, local honey, artisanal bread, handmade soaps, and much more. It's an excellent opportunity to support local farmers and artisans while enjoying the community atmosphere.

The Farm at RSLV: Located in nearby Henderson, The Farm at RSLV (formerly known as Gilcrease Orchard) is a delightful destination for picking your own fresh produce. Depending on the season, you can pick apples, peaches, strawberries, and a variety of vegetables. It's a fun and interactive experience, allowing you to connect directly with the land and enjoy the fruits of your labor.

As you plan your visit, be sure to check the market's operating hours and any seasonal variations. Enjoy the community spirit, discover new flavors, and bring a taste of Las Vegas back home with you.

Get ready to indulge in a shopping spree like no other as we continue our Las Vegas adventure in the next chapter. In Chapter 6, we'll uncover the city's natural wonders and outdoor escapades, proving that there's more to Las Vegas than just the glittering lights of the Strip!

CAÑONITA

Chapter 6:

Beyond the Neon: Day Trips and Outdoor Escapes

Welcome to Chapter 6 of your personalized guide to Las Vegas! In this chapter, we'll venture beyond the neon lights of the city and explore the natural wonders, engineering marvels, and thrilling outdoor activities that await just a short distance away.

Get ready to embark on unforgettable day trips and experience the breathtaking beauty that surrounds Las Vegas!

Natural Wonders: Discovering the Beauty Surrounding Las Vegas

While Las Vegas is known for its vibrant entertainment scene, it's also a gateway to stunning natural landscapes that will leave you in awe. Take a break from the hustle and bustle of the Strip and immerse yourself in the following natural wonders:

Red Rock Canyon National Conservation Area: Just a short drive west of Las Vegas, Red Rock Canyon offers a mesmerizing display of crimson cliffs, unique rock formations, and scenic hiking trails. Lace up your hiking boots and explore the picturesque landscapes that have been featured in movies and documentaries.

Valley of Fire State Park: Experience the surreal beauty of Valley of Fire, Nevada's oldest state park. Marvel at the fiery red sandstone formations, ancient petroglyphs, and panoramic vistas. With hiking trails that wind through stunning landscapes, this park is a photographer's dream.

Mount Charleston: Escape the desert heat and venture to the cool mountain oasis of Mount Charleston. Located only 35 miles northwest of Las Vegas, this alpine retreat offers opportunities for hiking, camping, and even skiing in the winter months.

Hoover Dam and Beyond: Unveiling Engineering Marvels

A visit to Las Vegas wouldn't be complete without exploring the engineering marvels in the area, with Hoover Dam being a prime example. Here are some must-visit destinations that showcase human ingenuity:

Hoover Dam: Marvel at the iconic Hoover Dam, a monumental feat of engineering that stands as a testament to human perseverance. Take a guided tour to learn about its fascinating history, explore the power plant, and witness the impressive views of the Colorado River and Lake Mead.

Lake Mead National Recreation Area: Extend your visit to Hoover Dam and enjoy the outdoor splendor of Lake Mead. This expansive reservoir offers opportunities for boating, fishing, swimming, and even scuba diving. Indulge in water-based adventures surrounded by stunning desert landscapes.

Hiking, Golfing, and Adventuring: Outdoor Activities for Thrill Seekers

If you're an outdoor enthusiast and crave adrenaline-pumping experiences, Las Vegas has plenty to offer. Engage in thrilling activities and make the most of the city's unique outdoor offerings:

Hiking in Bootleg Canyon: Strap on your hiking boots and head to Bootleg Canyon in nearby Boulder City. This rugged desert canyon is a haven for hikers and mountain bikers, with trails ranging from leisurely strolls to challenging adventures. Soak in breathtaking views as you navigate the desert terrain.

Golfing at Top-Rated Courses: Tee off at world-class golf courses scattered throughout the Las Vegas Valley. With lush fairways, scenic views, and challenging holes, golf enthusiasts will find plenty of opportunities to perfect their swing and enjoy the perfect round of golf. Consider playing a round at renowned courses like Shadow Creek, Cascata, or TPC Las Vegas.

These courses offer not only exceptional golfing experiences but also luxurious amenities, including professional caddies, state-of-the-art facilities, and stunning clubhouse views.

Adventure Tours: Seek thrills with adventurous activities like ATV tours, zip-lining, and helicopter rides. Experience the exhilaration of zooming through desert dunes, soaring over the iconic Strip, or zip-lining through picturesque canyons.

When looking to book adventure tours in Las Vegas, you have several options to choose from. Here are some reputable tour operators and platforms where you can book your desired adventure activities:

Pink Adventure Tours: Pink Adventure Tours specializes in off-road adventures and scenic tours in the Las Vegas area.

They offer thrilling ATV tours, guided hiking excursions, and even helicopter tours over the Grand Canyon. With their experienced guides and well-maintained vehicles, Pink Adventure Tours provides high-quality experiences for adventure seekers.

Las Vegas ATV Tours: If you're specifically interested in ATV tours, Las Vegas ATV Tours is a reputable operator to consider. They offer guided ATV adventures through the desert landscapes surrounding Las Vegas, providing an exhilarating and memorable experience. You can choose from various tour durations and difficulty levels, ensuring a customized adventure to suit your preferences.

Maverick Helicopters: For those seeking a helicopter ride or tour, Maverick Helicopters is a trusted company known for its scenic aerial experiences. They offer helicopter tours over the Las Vegas Strip, Grand Canyon, and other breathtaking locations. With their state-of-the-art helicopters and knowledgeable pilots, Maverick Helicopters provides a safe and unforgettable adventure.

When booking your adventure tour, it's advisable to check the availability, tour schedules, and any specific requirements or restrictions. Be sure to read reviews from previous customers to get a sense of the tour quality and customer satisfaction. Additionally, consider booking in advance, especially during peak seasons, to secure your preferred date and time.

As we conclude our exploration of day trips and outdoor escapes, remember to pack your sense of adventure and prepare for the unexpected. In the next chapter, we'll delve into the city's vibrant nightlife and offer recommendations for an unforgettable evening on the town!

Chapter 7:

Nighttime Revelries: Clubs, Bars, and Adult Entertainment

Welcome to Chapter 7 of your personalized guide to Las Vegas! As the sun sets, the city truly comes alive, offering a kaleidoscope of nightlife experiences.

In this chapter, we'll dive into the world of nighttime revelries, from pulsating nightclubs and trendy bars to expertly crafted cocktails and the sensational adult entertainment that Las Vegas is renowned for. Get ready to dance, sip, and explore the electrifying nightlife scene of Sin City!

Dance 'til Dawn: Hottest Nightclubs and Trendy Bars

Las Vegas is synonymous with unrivaled nightlife and world-class entertainment. Step into the glitz and glamour of the city's hottest nightclubs and trendy bars:

Omnia Nightclub: Experience the epitome of Vegas nightlife at Omnia, located in Caesars Palace. With its state-of-the-art sound system, mesmerizing light displays, and performances by renowned DJs, this multi-level nightclub offers an unforgettable party experience.

Location: Caesars Palace, 3570 S Las Vegas Blvd, Las Vegas, NV

XS Nightclub: Immerse yourself in luxury at XS, nestled in the Wynn Encore. This upscale nightclub features a stunning outdoor pool area and a dance floor pulsating with energy. Dance to the beats of top DJs while indulging in the opulent ambiance that defines Las Vegas nightlife.

Location: Wynn Las Vegas. 3131 Las Vegas Blvd S, Las Vegas, NV

The Chandelier: Step into The Chandelier, a unique bar experience located in The Cosmopolitan. Spanning three levels, this dazzling bar is encased in a massive chandelier, creating an enchanting atmosphere. Savor expertly crafted cocktails as you bask in the glamorous surroundings.

Location: The Cosmopolitan of Las Vegas. 3708 Las Vegas Blvd S, Las Vegas, NV

Mixology Magic: Craft Cocktails and Speakeasies

Las Vegas is home to an array of mixology magic, where talented bartenders push the boundaries of creativity. Discover hidden speakeasies and sample expertly crafted cocktails at these noteworthy establishments:

The Laundry Room: Embark on a secret drinking experience at The Laundry Room, a hidden speakeasy within Commonwealth. Make a reservation and step back in time as you sip on innovative cocktails in an intimate setting. This exclusive hideaway promises an unforgettable mixology adventure.

Location: 525 E Fremont St, Las Vegas, NV

Velveteen Rabbit: Unleash your inner cocktail connoisseur at Velveteen Rabbit, an eclectic bar in the Arts District.

Known for its imaginative libations, this cozy and artistic spot offers a vibrant atmosphere and a menu that celebrates local and seasonal ingredients.

Location: 1218 S Main St, Las Vegas, NV

The Dorsey: Located in The Venetian, The Dorsey is a sophisticated lounge known for its expertly mixed cocktails. With its chic design and impressive drink menu, this stylish destination is perfect for enjoying a classic cocktail or exploring unique flavor combinations.

Location: 3355 S Las Vegas Blvd #200 3355, Las Vegas

Naughty but Nice: Exploring Vegas' Sensational Adult Entertainment

Las Vegas is notorious for its adult entertainment, and if you're seeking an evening of risqué fun, these venues are sure to captivate your senses:

Absinthe: Prepare for a night of outrageous entertainment at Absinthe, a show that combines acrobatics, comedy, and daring acts. This saucy and exhilarating performance, held in a Spiegeltent at Caesars Palace, will leave you laughing and amazed.

Location: 3570 S Las Vegas Blvd, Las Vegas, NV

Fantasy: Experience a seductive and captivating show at Fantasy, performed at the Luxor. Featuring talented dancers, sultry costumes, and enticing choreography, this adult revue promises an evening of sensual entertainment.

Location: 3900 South Las Vegas Boulevard Luxor, Las Vegas, NV

Spearmint Rhino: For those seeking a more intimate experience, Spearmint Rhino Gentlemen's Club offers a luxurious and upscale atmosphere. With stunning performers and impeccable service, this renowned establishment sets the stage for an unforgettable night out.

Location: 3340 S Highland Dr, Las Vegas, NV

As we conclude our exploration of Las Vegas' vibrant nightlife, remember to let loose, embrace the energy of the city, and create memories that will last a lifetime. In the next chapter, we'll unveil the hidden gems and lesser-known attractions that will add a touch of adventure to your Las Vegas journey!

Chapter 8:

Hidden Gems and Lesser-Known Attractions: Unveiling Las Vegas' Best-Kept Secrets

Las Vegas is a city known for its glitz, glamour, and larger-than-life attractions. However, beyond the bright lights of the Strip, there are hidden gems and lesser-known treasures waiting to be discovered.

In this chapter, we'll delve into the secret side of Las Vegas, exploring off-the-beaten-path destinations that offer a unique and unforgettable experience. Get ready to uncover the hidden gems that make Las Vegas truly special.

The Neon Boneyard: A Time Capsule of Vegas History

Tucked away behind the scenes of the city's flashy facades lies the Neon Boneyard, a captivating open-air museum dedicated to preserving iconic Las Vegas signage from days gone by.

Take a guided tour through this neon graveyard and marvel at the vintage signs that once adorned the Strip. Each sign tells a story, reflecting the rich history and vibrant spirit of Las Vegas.

It's a must-visit destination for history buffs, photography enthusiasts, and anyone seeking a nostalgic glimpse into the city's past.

Location: 770 Las Vegas Blvd N, Las Vegas, NV

The Pinball Hall of Fame: Gaming with a Retro Twist

Step back in time and immerse yourself in a world of flashing lights, ringing bells, and nostalgic arcade games at the Pinball Hall of Fame. This hidden gem houses one of the largest collections of pinball machines in the world.

From vintage classics to modern favorites, you can spend hours flipping and tilting your way through rows of colorful pinball machines. Not only is it a fun-filled experience for all ages, but it's also a nonprofit organization, with proceeds going to charity.

Location: 4925 Las Vegas Blvd S, Las Vegas, NV

The Downtown Container Park: Where Creativity Meets Entertainment

Nestled in the heart of downtown Las Vegas, the Container Park is a unique shopping, dining, and entertainment destination. This open-air mall is constructed entirely from repurposed shipping containers, creating a vibrant and eco-friendly atmosphere.

Stroll through the diverse boutiques, savor delectable bites from food vendors, and enjoy live performances on the central stage. The Container Park offers a refreshing break from the hustle and bustle of the Strip, showcasing the city's creative side.

Location: 707 E Fremont St, Las Vegas, NV

The Valley of Fire State Park: Nature's Masterpiece

Escape the glitz of the city and venture to the nearby Valley of Fire State Park, where nature reigns supreme.

This hidden gem boasts stunning red sandstone formations, ancient petroglyphs, and breathtaking vistas that make it a paradise for outdoor enthusiasts.

Hike through vibrant desert trails, marvel at the unique rock formations, and witness the fiery colors that give the park its name. Don't forget your camera, as the Valley of Fire offers countless opportunities for awe-inspiring photographs.

As you explore Las Vegas, don't confine yourself to the well-known attractions. Take the time to seek out these hidden gems and lesser-known attractions that offer a different perspective on the city.

Whether you're immersing yourself in the nostalgic charm of the Neon Boneyard, reliving the arcade days at the Pinball Hall of Fame, enjoying the creative ambiance of the Downtown Container Park, or discovering the natural wonders of the Valley of Fire State Park, these hidden gems will add an extra layer of intrigue and excitement to your Las Vegas adventure.

Chapter 9:

Family-Friendly Fun: Las Vegas for All Ages

Contrary to popular belief, Las Vegas isn't just for adults—it's a destination that offers a wealth of family-friendly attractions and entertainment. In this chapter, we'll explore the diverse array of activities that will keep both kids and adults entertained. Get ready for a memorable and inclusive adventure in the entertainment capital of the world!

From Arcade Bliss to Theme Park Thrills: Kid-Friendly Attractions

Las Vegas boasts an array of attractions and a variety of interactive museums and educational adventures that blend entertainment with learning and cater specifically to the younger crowd.

Delight in these family-friendly experiences that are sure to create lasting memories:

Adventuredome at Circus Circus: Step into a world of excitement and adventure at Adventuredome, an indoor theme park located at Circus Circus. From thrilling rides and roller coasters to arcade games and mini-golf, there's something for everyone in the family to enjoy.

Discovery Children's Museum: Ignite your child's curiosity at the Discovery Children's Museum, a hands-on learning wonderland. With interactive exhibits and educational programs spanning science, art, and culture, this museum will spark imaginations and engage young minds.

Shark Reef Aquarium at Mandalay Bay: Immerse yourself in an underwater world at the Shark Reef Aquarium. Marvel at a diverse range of marine life, including sharks, stingrays, and tropical fish. The interactive touch pools and educational presentations make this a captivating experience for all ages.

The Mob Museum: Dive into the intriguing world of organized crime at The Mob Museum.

Through immersive exhibits and interactive displays, learn about the history of the mob and its impact on Las Vegas and beyond. This thought-provoking museum provides an engaging experience for visitors of all ages.

Springs Preserve: Embark on an educational journey through the Springs Preserve, a 180-acre nature preserve and cultural center. Discover the rich history, diverse wildlife, and sustainable practices of the Mojave Desert through exhibits, botanical gardens, and informative presentations.

Shows, Magic, and Marvels: Entertainment for the Whole Family

Las Vegas is renowned for its world-class entertainment, and there are shows and performances that cater specifically to a family audience. Enjoy these family-friendly spectacles that will leave you in awe:

Cirque du Soleil Shows: Immerse yourself in the enchanting world of Cirque du Soleil, known for its breathtaking acrobatics and mesmerizing performances.

From "Mystère" at Treasure Island to "The Beatles LOVE" at The Mirage, these shows offer a feast for the senses and captivate audiences of all ages.

Mac King Comedy Magic Show: Prepare for an afternoon of laughter and magic at the Mac King Comedy Magic Show, held at Harrah's Las Vegas. This hilarious and interactive performance combines mind-boggling illusions with comedic wit, creating an unforgettable experience for the whole family.

Tournament of Kings: Transport yourself to the medieval era at the Tournament of Kings, a dinner show at Excalibur. Watch knights jousting, cheer for your kingdom, and indulge in a hearty meal fit for royalty. This thrilling and immersive show provides an exciting experience for children and adults alike.

In the final chapter, we'll uncover some amazing retreats where you can relax and rejuvenate before you say goodbye to Las Vegas. You'll also find some additional tips and recommendations to ensure your Las Vegas adventure is truly unforgettable!

Chapter 10:

Relaxation and Rejuvenation: Spas and Wellness Retreats

Welcome to the final chapter of your personalized guide to Las Vegas! Amidst the exhilarating energy of the city, it's important to find moments of relaxation and rejuvenation.

In this chapter, we'll explore the world of spas and wellness retreats, where you can indulge in pampering treatments, find your inner balance, and nourish your mind, body, and soul. Get ready to unwind and discover the oasis of tranquility that awaits you in the heart of Las Vegas!

Pampering Paradise: Luxurious Spas for Ultimate Relaxation

Las Vegas is home to a plethora of world-class spas that offer luxurious treatments and serene environments. Treat yourself to the following pampering paradises:

The Spa at Encore: Step into a haven of tranquility at The Spa at Encore, located in the Wynn Encore resort. With its opulent decor and a wide range of indulgent treatments, including massages, facials, and body wraps, this spa promises an unforgettable pampering experience.

Sahra Spa & Hammam at The Cosmopolitan: Escape to a Moroccan-inspired sanctuary at Sahra Spa & Hammam. Unwind in the steam rooms, rejuvenate with a massage, or indulge in a soothing body treatment. The serene ambiance and attention to detail make this spa a true oasis of relaxation.

Qua Baths & Spa at Caesars Palace: Immerse yourself in a Roman-inspired retreat at Qua Baths & Spa. From their signature Roman Baths to invigorating hydrotherapy treatments, this award-winning spa offers a rejuvenating experience that will leave you feeling refreshed and revitalized.

Yoga Retreats and Fitness Centers: Staying Active in Sin City

Maintaining your wellness routine is made easy in Las Vegas, with a variety of yoga retreats and fitness centers that cater to all levels of practice. Stay active and centered at these notable venues:

TruFusion: Elevate your fitness journey at TruFusion, a premier fitness studio offering a variety of classes, including yoga, Pilates, barre, and more. With a welcoming and vibrant atmosphere, TruFusion is the perfect place to break a sweat and find your inner strength. They have multiple location in the city so you can choose whichever's closest to you.

Shine Alternative Fitness: Embark on a unique fitness adventure at Shine Alternative Fitness, where you can explore aerial arts, pole dancing, and other innovative workout options. Challenge your body, boost your confidence, and have fun in this empowering fitness space.

Silent Savasana: Experience the serenity of Silent Savasana, a unique outdoor yoga experience that takes place in iconic Las Vegas locations. Don wireless headphones and immerse yourself in a guided yoga practice while enjoying breathtaking views. This unforgettable yoga session combines mindfulness, movement, and the vibrant energy of the city.

Recharging Your Batteries: Mindfulness and Wellness Experiences

Las Vegas offers a range of mindfulness and wellness experiences that promote relaxation, self-care, and personal growth. Discover these recharging opportunities:

The Grand Spa at MGM Grand: Escape the hustle and bustle of the Strip and find serenity at The Grand Spa. From meditation classes to energy healing sessions, this spa embraces holistic wellness practices, allowing you to recharge and restore balance to your life.

The Neon Museum: Take a break from the city's fast pace and immerse yourself in the unique serenity of The Neon Museum. Stroll through the outdoor exhibition of vintage neon signs, learn about the city's history, and find inspiration in the artistry of the past.

Float Centers: Experience the ultimate relaxation at a float center, where you can float effortlessly in a sensory deprivation tank filled with saltwater. Let go of external stimuli, quiet your mind, and embrace a state of deep relaxation and rejuvenation. There are a handful of them in the city with a good reputation. I'll recommend NV Float Therapy at 2291 S Fort Apache Rd.

As we conclude our exploration of relaxation and rejuvenation in Las Vegas, remember to take time for self-care and well-being during your visit. In the conclusion, we'll wrap up our guide with some additional tips and recommendations to ensure your Las Vegas experience is truly unforgettable!

Conclusion:

Leaving Las Vegas with Unforgettable Memories

As we come to the end of this personalized guide to Las Vegas, it's time to reflect on the incredible experiences and memories you've created during your visit. Las Vegas is a city like no other, where the glitz, glamour, and vibrant energy combine to create a truly unforgettable destination.

Whether you've explored the iconic Strip, reveled in world-class entertainment, indulged in exquisite dining, or discovered the hidden gems beyond the neon lights, you've undoubtedly immersed yourself in the magic of this extraordinary city.

As you prepare to leave Las Vegas, remember to take a moment to appreciate the memories you've made. Cherish the laughter shared, the adventures embarked upon, and the moments of awe and wonder that have left an indelible mark on your journey.

The spirit of Las Vegas will stay with you long after you depart, reminding you of the excitement, the thrill, and the joy that you experienced during your time here.

But Las Vegas isn't just a destination—it's a mindset. Carry the spirit of Las Vegas with you wherever you go, embracing the daring, the bold, and the limitless possibilities that life has to offer. Allow the energy of this city to inspire you to take risks, follow your passions, and create your own extraordinary moments, wherever your travels may take you next.

As you bid farewell to Las Vegas, remember to extend gratitude to the incredible individuals who have contributed to your experience—the welcoming locals, the talented performers, the dedicated service staff, and the visionaries who continue to shape and reinvent this remarkable city.

On behalf of all the extraordinary entertainment, shimmering neon lights and the overall amazingness of Sin City, I hope this journey has exceeded your expectations.

May your memories of Las Vegas be etched in your heart, and may you carry the spirit of this city with you always.

Safe travels, and may your future adventures be filled with excitement, wonder, and unforgettable moments!

Farewell, and until we meet again in another exciting destination!

- D.D

Appendix:

Practical Information and Resources

In this appendix, you'll find practical information and resources to enhance your Las Vegas experience. From accommodation options to staying safe and navigating seasonal events and festivals, this section will provide you with valuable insights and resources to make the most of your visit.

Where to Stay: Hotels, Resorts, and Unique Accommodations

Las Vegas offers a vast array of accommodation options to suit every taste and budget. Whether you prefer the luxury of world-renowned resorts, the convenience of hotels on the Strip, or the charm of boutique accommodations, you'll find a perfect place to rest and recharge.

As a visitor to Las Vegas, you have a range of accommodation options to choose from, whether you're seeking luxury or budget-friendly options. Here are some recommendations:

Luxury Hotel Options:

The Venetian Resort: Experience opulence at The Venetian, a lavish resort offering spacious suites, world-class dining, and a replica of Venice's Grand Canal complete with gondola rides.

Bellagio Las Vegas: Indulge in luxury at Bellagio, known for its elegant rooms, stunning fountain shows, and exquisite dining options, including the renowned Picasso restaurant.

Wynn Las Vegas: Immerse yourself in luxury at Wynn Las Vegas, featuring high-end accommodations, a tranquil spa, and exceptional dining experiences like the Michelin-starred restaurant, Wing Lei.

Budget-Friendly Options:

Excalibur Hotel & Casino: Stay at Excalibur, a castle-themed hotel that offers affordable rooms, various dining options, and entertainment like the Tournament of Kings dinner show.

The LINQ Hotel + Experience: Enjoy a modern and affordable stay at The LINQ, centrally located on the Strip. This hotel offers comfortable rooms, a vibrant casino, and easy access to The LINQ Promenade.

Circus Circus Hotel, Casino & Theme Park: Perfect for families or budget-conscious travelers, Circus Circus provides affordable rooms, an indoor amusement park, and circus performances.

Additionally, consider checking for deals and discounts through hotel booking websites or signing up for hotel loyalty programs, as they can provide exclusive rates and perks.

Keep in mind that Las Vegas is a popular destination, so prices may vary depending on the season and demand. It's advisable to book your accommodations well in advance, especially if you're planning to visit during peak times or major events.

Also, consider factors such as location, amenities, and proximity to attractions when choosing your accommodation. Websites and travel booking platforms can assist you in finding the best deals and comparing options based on your preferences.

Essential Tips for Staying Safe and Avoiding Common Pitfalls

While Las Vegas is generally a safe destination, it's important to take necessary precautions to ensure a smooth and secure visit. Here are some essential tips to keep in mind:

- Stay alert and aware of your surroundings, particularly in crowded areas.
- Use designated crosswalks when navigating busy streets.

- Keep your personal belongings secure and be mindful of your valuables.
- Avoid walking alone late at night, especially in unfamiliar areas.
- Use reputable transportation options such as licensed taxis or ride-sharing services.
- Familiarize yourself with emergency contact numbers and the location of nearby medical facilities.
- Remember, your safety is paramount, so trust your instincts and exercise caution throughout your Las Vegas adventure.

Seasonal Events and Festivals: Making the Most of Your Visit

Las Vegas is known for its vibrant events and festivals that take place throughout the year. Whether you're interested in music, culture, sports, or culinary delights, there's always something happening in the city.

Here are some seasonal events and festivals that you shouldn't miss during your visit:

Chinese New Year Celebration: Embrace the vibrant energy of Chinese New Year in Las Vegas, where the city comes alive with festivities. The famous Bellagio Conservatory and Botanical Gardens showcases a stunning display featuring traditional Chinese decorations, including giant dragon sculptures and blooming cherry blossoms. Enjoy cultural performances, dragon dances, and indulge in special Chinese cuisine offerings at various restaurants.

St. Patrick's Day Parade: Every March, Las Vegas transforms into a sea of green to celebrate St. Patrick's Day. The annual St. Patrick's Day Parade winds its way through the city, featuring elaborate floats, marching bands, and spirited participants dressed in green. Join the revelry, don your best green attire, and enjoy the lively atmosphere and traditional Irish music and dancing.

Electric Daisy Carnival (EDC): Held in May, the Electric Daisy Carnival is a world-renowned electronic dance music festival that takes over the Las Vegas Motor Speedway for a weekend of non-stop music, art installations, and electrifying performances.

Join the crowd of enthusiastic music lovers, dance to the beats of renowned DJs, and experience the incredible visual spectacles that make EDC an unforgettable event.

Fourth of July Fireworks: Celebrate America's Independence Day with spectacular fireworks display in Las Vegas. Various locations along the Strip, including Caesars Palace, the Stratosphere, and Mandalay Bay, put on dazzling pyrotechnic shows, lighting up the night sky. Find a prime viewing spot, grab a picnic blanket, and enjoy the patriotic ambiance and breathtaking fireworks extravaganza.

Life is Beautiful Festival: In September, immerse yourself in the vibrant atmosphere of the Life is Beautiful Festival. This multi-day event celebrates music, art, and food, with a diverse lineup of musicians, interactive art installations, and renowned culinary offerings. Explore the festival grounds, discover emerging artists, indulge in gourmet bites, and soak in the creative energy that permeates the event.

Las Vegas Pride: Join the LGBTQ+ community and allies in celebrating diversity and equality at Las Vegas Pride, held in October. The festival includes a colorful parade, live entertainment, vendor booths, and a vibrant street fair. Show your support, participate in the festivities, and embrace the inclusive spirit of Las Vegas.

These are just a few examples of the seasonal events and festivals that take place in Las Vegas. Make sure to check the dates and specific details for each event before planning your visit.

Stay informed about upcoming events and plan your visit accordingly to add an extra layer of excitement to your trip. Check official event websites and local event listings for the most up-to-date information on dates, venues, and ticket availability.

Additionally, be aware of seasonal considerations such as weather conditions and peak tourist periods. Las Vegas can be quite hot during the summer months, so pack accordingly and stay hydrated. Spring and fall tend to offer milder temperatures, making it an ideal time to explore outdoor attractions and enjoy al fresco dining.

Best Times to Travel:

Las Vegas experiences a desert climate, characterized by hot summers and mild winters. Consider these factors when planning your trip:

Spring (March to May) and fall (September to November) offer pleasant temperatures, making them ideal for outdoor activities and exploring the city. These seasons also tend to be less crowded, allowing you to enjoy attractions with fewer crowds.

If you can handle the heat, summer (June to August) offers a vibrant atmosphere with pool parties, outdoor concerts, and longer daylight hours. Be prepared for high temperatures and plan indoor activities during the hottest parts of the day.

Winter (December to February) brings cooler temperatures but remains mild compared to many other parts of the country. This is a great time to take advantage of lower hotel rates and enjoy indoor entertainment options.

The best time to visit Las Vegas largely depends on your preferences. Spring and fall offer milder temperatures and are generally considered more comfortable for outdoor activities. However, if you enjoy the heat and want to experience pool parties and other summertime events, then summer could be the ideal time for you.

It's important to note that Las Vegas is a popular destination year-round, so expect crowds and higher hotel rates during peak seasons and major events. Consider planning your visit during weekdays or shoulder seasons for a more relaxed experience.

With the practical information and resources provided in this appendix, you'll be equipped to make informed decisions and optimize your Las Vegas experience. Whether you're seeking accommodation, prioritizing your safety, or looking to attend exciting events, remember to utilize reliable sources, plan ahead, and remain open to the unexpected adventures that Las Vegas has in store for you.

Safe travels and may your time in Las Vegas be filled with excitement, joy, and cherished memories!

Printed in Great Britain
by Amazon

25443056R00053